At the MARSH in the MEADOW

Jeanie Mebane • illustrated by Gerald Guerlais

PUBLISHED BY SLEEPING BEAR PRESS

This is the marsh
In the middle of the meadow.

This is the **mucky mud**
On the bottom of the **marsh**
In the middle of the **meadow**.

These are the reeds

That grow in the **mucky mud**

On the bottom of the **marsh**

In the middle of the **meadow**.

These are tiny algae
    That float among the reeds
        That grow in the mucky mud
    On the bottom of the marsh
In the middle of the meadow.

These are little mayflies
That gobble tiny **algae**
That float among the **reeds**
That grow in the **mucky mud**
On the bottom of the **marsh**
In the middle of the **meadow**.

These are water spiders

That snag little mayflies

That gobble tiny algae

That float among the reeds

That grow in the mucky mud

On the bottom of the marsh

In the middle of the meadow.

These are the dragonflies

That nibble **water spiders**

That snag little **mayflies**

That gobble tiny **algae**

That float among the **reeds**

That grow in the **mucky mud**

On the bottom of the **marsh**

In the middle of the **meadow**.

These are the minnows

That dine on the **dragonflies**

That nibble **water spiders**

That snag little **mayflies**

That gobble tiny **algae**

That float among the **reeds**

That grow in the **mucky mud**

On the bottom of the **marsh**

In the middle of the **meadow**.

These are the tadpoles
That slurp up the **minnows**
That dine on the **dragonflies**
That nibble **water spiders**
That snag little **mayflies**
That gobble tiny **algae**
That float among the **reeds**
That grow in the **mucky mud**
On the bottom of the **marsh**
In the middle of the **meadow**.

These are the fish

That gulp down the **tadpoles**

That slurp up the **minnows**

That dine on the **dragonflies**

That nibble **water spiders**

That snag little **mayflies**

That gobble tiny **algae**

That float among the **reeds**

That grow in the **mucky mud**

On the bottom of the **marsh**

In the middle of the **meadow.**

This is the **big eagle**
That swoops from up high
To grasp the **fish**
That gulp down the **tadpoles**
That slurp up the **minnows**
That dine on the **dragonflies**

That nibble **water spiders**

That snag little **mayflies**

That gobble tiny **algae**

That float among the **reeds**

That grow in the **mucky mud**

On the bottom of the **marsh**

In the middle of the **meadow**.

These are the

Fed by the **big eagle**

That swoops from up high

To grasp the **fish**

That gulp down the **tadpoles**

That slurp up the **minnows**

That dine on the **dragonflies**

That nibble **water spiders**

That snag little **mayflies**

That gobble tiny **algae**

That float among the **reeds**

That grow in the **mucky mud**

On the bottom of the **marsh**

In the middle of the **meadow**.

From
reeds to algae
mayflies to spiders
dragonflies to minnows

tadpoles to fish
eagle to eaglets,
the marsh in the meadow
nourishes them all.

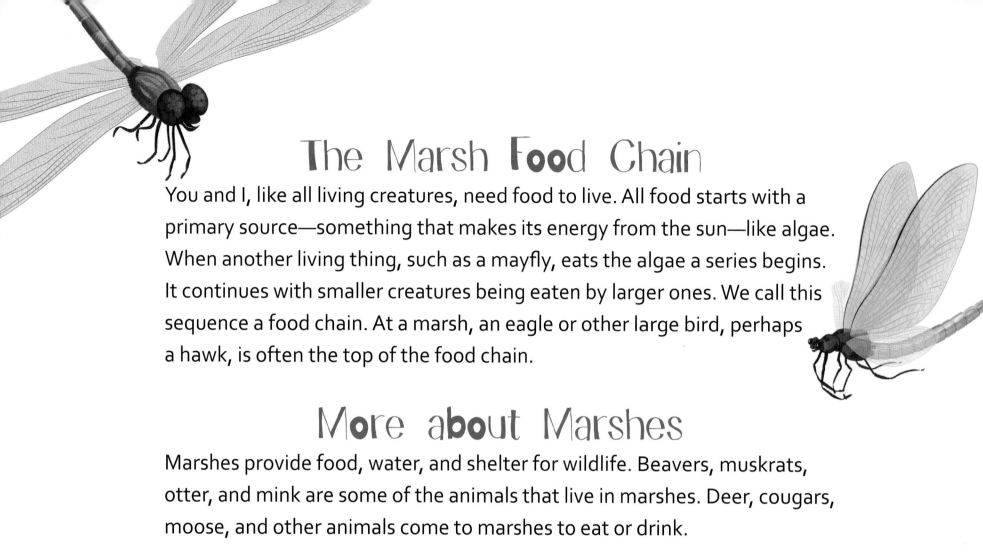

The Marsh Food Chain

You and I, like all living creatures, need food to live. All food starts with a primary source—something that makes its energy from the sun—like algae. When another living thing, such as a mayfly, eats the algae a series begins. It continues with smaller creatures being eaten by larger ones. We call this sequence a food chain. At a marsh, an eagle or other large bird, perhaps a hawk, is often the top of the food chain.

More about Marshes

Marshes provide food, water, and shelter for wildlife. Beavers, muskrats, otter, and mink are some of the animals that live in marshes. Deer, cougars, moose, and other animals come to marshes to eat or drink.

Over 90 percent of all birds need marshes or another type of wetlands to survive. Some birds, including ducks, coots, and geese, live in marshes. Other birds such as herons, snipes, and cranes live near marshes and feed in them. Birds that migrate seek marshes as places to rest and eat while migrating.

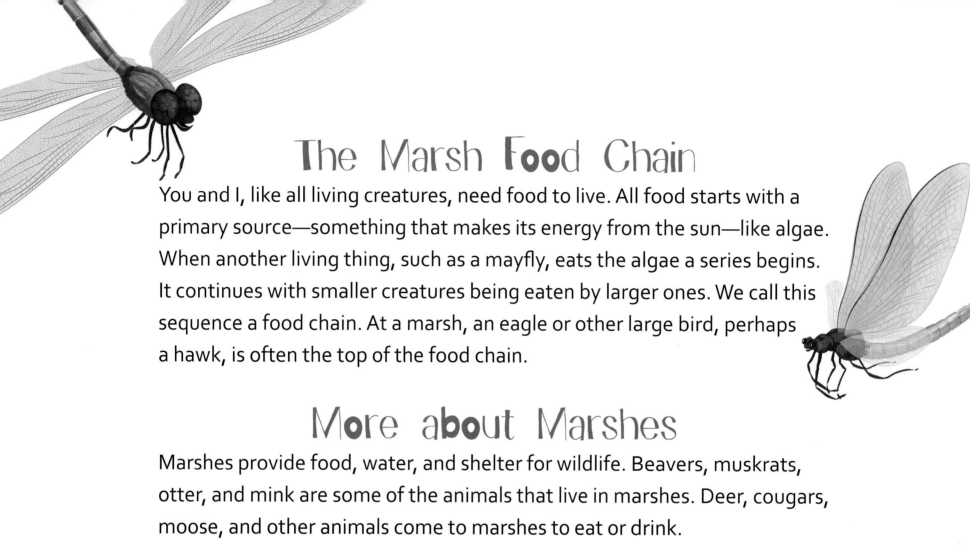

The Marsh Food Chain

You and I, like all living creatures, need food to live. All food starts with a primary source—something that makes its energy from the sun—like algae. When another living thing, such as a mayfly, eats the algae a series begins. It continues with smaller creatures being eaten by larger ones. We call this sequence a food chain. At a marsh, an eagle or other large bird, perhaps a hawk, is often the top of the food chain.

More about Marshes

Marshes provide food, water, and shelter for wildlife. Beavers, muskrats, otter, and mink are some of the animals that live in marshes. Deer, cougars, moose, and other animals come to marshes to eat or drink.

Over 90 percent of all birds need marshes or another type of wetlands to survive. Some birds, including ducks, coots, and geese, live in marshes. Other birds such as herons, snipes, and cranes live near marshes and feed in them. Birds that migrate seek marshes as places to rest and eat while migrating.

Glossary

Algae—a form of plants without roots, stems, or leaves, that mainly live in water. In marshes, algae are usually tiny and may look like scum.

Dragonflies—insects with slender bodies, big eyes, and two pairs of see-through wings. Dragonflies are larger than most other insects and can fly very fast. Dragonflies eat lots of mosquitoes as well as other insects.

Eagles—large birds that primarily feed on fish. Eagles nest in tall trees or high cliffs near water. An eagle can swoop down to the water and grab a fish without landing. Holding the fish in its strong talons, the eagle flies back to its nest or another safe perch where it either eats the fish or gives it to its young.

Marsh—Low, wet land with small grassy reeds and other plants. Water in a marsh can vary from a few inches to a few feet deep. Saltwater marshes form in low-lying coastal areas while freshwater marshes are in low inland sites.

Mayflies—small insects with delicate wings. Mayflies live only two or three days.

Minnows—small, slender fish only a few inches long. Minnows eat aquatic insects and even tiny water plants.

Reeds—tall plants with straight stems that grow in marshy places.

Tadpoles—the very young form of frogs and toads. Young tadpoles have tails and eat plant material. As they develop they seek meatlike food such as pond worms and small minnows.

Water spiders—commonly used title for large spiders that run across the water in ponds and streams to catch and eat water insects.

To Chris, Ann, Melissa, and all children
who wonder at the world around them.

—Jeanie

To all kids who love spending hours observing bugs, animals,
and all the wonders of the greatest artist: Mother Nature.

—Gerald

Sleeping Bear Press™

2395 South Huron Parkway, Suite 200, Ann Arbor, MI 48104
www.sleepingbearpress.com
© Sleeping Bear Press

Printed and bound in the United States.
10 9 8 7 6 5 4 3 2 1

ISBN: 978-1-58536-958-4

Library of Congress Cataloging-in-Publication Data
Names: Mebane, Jeanie, author. | Guerlais, Gerald, illustrator.
Title: At the marsh in the meadow / written by Jeanie Mebane ; illustrator, Gerald Guerlais.
Description: Ann Arbor, MI : Sleeping Bear Press, [2016]
Identifiers: LCCN 2015027639 | ISBN 9781585369584
Subjects: LCSH: Wetlands—Juvenile literature. | Wetland ecology—Juvenile literature
Classification: LCC QH541.5.M3 M43 2016 | DDC 577.68—dc23
LC record available at http://lccn.loc.gov/2015027639